Table of Contents

DEDICATION 2

Table of Contents 3

Love, Begins **5**

Worth It...6

Goals...7

Forever Mine 8

Missing That 9

Waves Pounding 10

Alive Again 11

Nobody Else..14

Can't With You 16

Emotions of the Time...18

Eternity Moments...20

Naked Emotions..22

My Only Weapon..24

Love There..26

Love, Tested..**28**

The Real You...29

That's Right...31

My Eye 33

Here Together 34

For You..35

Keeping On 37

New Season 39

Be Still...41

Love, In The Small Things 43

    Selective Times...44

    Like That...45

    Owned Time...46

    A Gift..47

Us, Against the World **48**

    Gone Home..49

    We Are Ready...51

    Took Risks 52

Love, In The War Room **54**

    That Existence 55

    Means and Ends...56

    Battle Cry 57

    Went There 59

    Don't Worry 61

    Something Special...63

    Closer to You 65

    Only Gain 66

    Your Reward 68

Love, Established..**70**

    Open Minded 71

    We Grew 72

    ABOUT THE AUTHOR......................................76

DEDICATION

My wife, Candace Lockett

EBOOK ISBN: 978-1-7345651-0-2
PAPERBACK ISBN: 978-1-7345651-1-9

Library of Congress Control Number : 8476627800

ATTENTION: SCHOOLS AND BUSINESSES
Dream Compound Books are available at quantity discounts with bulk purchase for educational, business, or sales promotional use. For information, please email the Dream Compound Team at info@dreamcompoundprods.com

INDIVIDUALS: Get Clarence Lockett's Second Poetry Book, Everybody Talking, Prove Your Word, for FREE

Sign up for the no-spam newsletter and get it when enter your email address.

Details can be found at the end of Through Mud and Water.

LOVE, BEGINS

Worth It

I lived this life trying to find a special

feeling. Someone to give my effort to.

It was machines and false hopes before

I knew you. But you fulfilled me with something

real again. To have your heat next to me

that grew me like the plants in the fields. To feel

wanted again, given time, energy, focus all

for me to give it back felt like I was on

the right cycle again. I almost lost all hope

on finding someone -- it was all a silly game

I had given up on playing. But you came

like fresh spring water after an exhausting run.

Goals

When I first met you, I thought what kind of man am I

and what kind of man can she make me to be?

Forever Mine

Yes, there were as many options available

as sand in the sea, but I knew exactly what

I desired. I persisted to have you in so many

inventive ways it was a matter of when, not

if I would have you. And when that day came,

mercy, mercy. You would know how it would feel

to be immersed into a sea of desire. If every

move was calculating and methodical before,

now you would be initiated into a sequence

of charms, dreams, and feelings so deep,

you will drown in them. Every step I will go

to execute the minor details and big picture

of this plan. To let you know how serious I am

about everything I do for you. I will sit you on

the bed, grabbing your hand, kneeling before

you and declaring everything you mean

to me with the sweetest touch and kisses to your hand.

Missing That

This time it will be perfect. You were shy at first,

but I knew what I wanted. All of you was shining

like a golden star. And you were to be handled with care. I

saw the vision of us together at that first encounter. At the

first conversation, there was that silence that said more

than words ever could. Those unseen forces were moving

about, yes, I knew there was unspent energy building. But

I waited, and let things flow naturally. Once you were in

my sight, the moment just right, you fell into my embrace.

I would know you, study you, it was all fierce passion that

had its peaks and valleys. Exploring your unknowns,

seeing you highlights. In awe of it all, savoring it. Having

gratitude of those moments. Being that lucky guy. I had to

be away, but I despised those times.

Waves Pounding

Can I kneel in this place looking into your eyes,

saying these words? Moving my finger tips

across your thighs for the first time. I

persisted to get to know you, barriers

were up like walls on a great castle,

but I found a way into your kingdom. We

must bond in a way that cherishes every

moment. Let us savor every step like

they were our last few breaths. Let me

stare at you, memorizing every perfect

part about you. Let us embrace like the

sea with the rocks of the sea shore.

Let our love lift up like that sea water

that bursts into the air.

Alive Again

I had become numb to the routine but your eyes,

gripping your thighs and holding you close brought

me life again. I felt numb to the nosies, dead to the

Internet and its insanity but those Sunday rides,

just you and I made me feel alive again. I had begun

to suffer and called the whole world a motherfucker

but something about you and your smile brought

me alive again. Can I live this life with these cloaks

of mystery and masks, fearing the reactions, or will

I live freely like your love will have me, without a

care or thought about how to be? I will live freely

til they blow this motherfucker up and we

are resurrected again. Then I hope to love you again.

Change nothing, same hugs, kisses

again, same hopes, dreams, moments again.

What I know of you is so familiar I just hope those

two worlds blend. I know you again and what wasn't

real becomes real again, and you become my reality

and we can begin again.

I love you til eternity.

Nobody Else

Can I ask for anybody else but you?

Your questions of insecurity belong to

that other fellow, but I got his inheritance

of ingratitude. What you thought was, I

might be like him but I will defy the odds

to gain your trust. These actions speak

louder than words so please watch my

every move. See, I don't lack character, I

am one built from lifelong commitments.

If I say it, I will do it, even if I am deprived

of a pot to piss in. Never has he gotten

uncomfortable for you, sacrificed this much

because he never knew he gained this

much to lose. I was given this man's

responsibility as a boy, and even then

I filled a man's shoes. What I am wanting

to tell you is there are no compromises

when I say I want you. A million other

women can approach but these eyes

won't ever leave you.

Can't With You

Summer's eve kissed you - you are a

pleasure to love. Long, billowing laughs

fill the walls and love is in your eyes.

It was all at ease. That smile filling

my soul like a glass of orange juice.

I can't with you.

I can't with you unless

I can have all of you.

This is what I dreamed of. You and your

happiness and your madness in our dream home.

I had known you for your actions and chose you

from that, so you were already morally right.

I got to see you and you blessed my sight.

Light talk weighed heavy on my soul, you

said so little but had an old soul. You

could not have known I did not like

fancy dinner dates and preferred the
backyard BBQs with friends. You could
not have known I loved the adventurous
life and you wanted to be different and
take risks with me again and again.
You could not have known how how
real this would feel and how I would
fall head over heels in love with you,
your essence, and we would live a life
of blessings. Call the reverend.
Let's get married today. No, I ain't
playing. I'm saying forget all the
fancy stuff. It's about our love.
We can do it for the public later,
let's do it for our love now. I have
never been so sure of nothing in my life.

Emotions of the Time

It was so quiet in this place without

your silk voice to echo off the walls.

This didn't feel like the summertime

I knew with all the noises. Grills,

spilling drinks into that glass,

laughter, kids wild, house with

that mild heat, A/C struggling to

keep up. The elders making sure

everybody got something to eat as

sure and demanding as when your

body demand you sleep. This was

the emotions of this time - all the

rage, fury, and excitement of

family visits with so many people in one place.

Eternity Moments

Oh, at last. The memories that woke me

at night were those that blew the candle out.

That light snuffed out like fireworks on

July fifth. At last, these memories came

like a lighted past of hills, music, and

fun with friends or family. A few fingers

playing that tune again that made our

heart dance. At the seashore, it was joy,

laughter as we made our steps and

movements. The sweet smell of those

flowers there, and the joy of that

exploration. That innocence restored

like spring leaves with sunlight shining

through them. The texture and distinct

taste of that food. These were those looks

that sparked an unspoken truth that

made us burst with joy. The brightness

there shining with all of its glory, these

were the days of the summer I spent

with you. These were the times that

lasted for a moment

but felt like an eternity.

Naked Emotions

A temporal gift of unequal measure was

the test of time I could give you no gift

that could meet these love standards

I set for you. Couldn't quite believe this

was the era of time we shared our life.

At this moment of noise, danger, and

unmet reconciliation, It was you and I

with a focus on each other that could

allow us to sustain for eternity. Our

commitment is a thoroughly woven quilt,

for warmth, for covering us in times of

sorrow. The time is now for our love

and has been for as long as I can

remember. The thoughts, dreams,

the acts, and even the fears we shared

were all part of this golden opportunity

to live unapologetically. The
understanding surpassing that
of the scribes, the wisdom of that
greater than the wise man, this was
two complete, unity. Our hearts
completely open, our emotions naked,
without a motive or intention, I set out
to know you. On these levels I came
to serve you in the best ways. Our gains
had surpassed any potential setbacks
in the past. This now is all I remembered
now. The bliss of this. As I experience this
new lightness of life, the power of the
moment surpassing anything I have
ever felt before, I experience you all
anew and we live as we knew
nothing again.

My Only Weapon

So early in the day, I haven't drawn

an inspiration for living, then I saw you.

Something about that smile exposed

my feelings and wrecks any vehicles

of stress or depression and puts me

in a transportation that's above buildings,

flying. I am not boxed in anymore. You

kept me on high. Can't believe so much

excitement can be had in a single being,

can't conceive not making a few carbon

copies of our combination connection.

Baby, I'm sure the one man that lost you

feeling like he lost his only weapon

in a world at war. Know there's ills from

your past, let me restore you like an

outdated PC. Those were mistakes a

boy made, let me hear you say I will

let this man take care of me. And I will, love.

Love There

My soul was unaware of the specifics.

The way we loved burned a hole

through my heart a dozen times.

Yes, it's hard to pin down love in

this world full of quiet interiors and

noisy exteriors. But I saw it in you.

Like a harp in a peaceful place,

drawn to you. You were open like

you'd never been hurt - trust there

from day one. The wind brought us

together, God made us meant to be.

I held you like I would never let go.

Time never changed us - loving you

with the flaws and all - you were still

perfect to me. The moonlight reflecting

off your delicate face was all I needed

for my heart to race. The work was

worth every sweat if it meant you would

be provided for. Learning you made this

life worth living. I had a PhD on progress

from knowing your favorite things, dislikes,

and preferences to where your best

massage spots were. I can't say any more than that I

am forever grateful God placed you in

the spot at that time that I met you.

LOVE, TESTED

The Real You

Love forgery. Our love lapsed at

ten thirty two pm. From a third

person I couldn't see them, this, us

Perception was off, tilted to the

left so I didn't know you. Slanted eyes,

you were Asian but you hid your whole

culture. Simple tasks made complicated

by your impossible mind. Off days ruined

because you don't know how to handle time.

What was this, so much invested, rather gambled,

we looked like a bad deal. I love you and hate you at the

same time.

I only say this because our love killed, murdered,

homicide what we decided.

I was ready to go and you would wait to argue because

you was complicated and I was simple.

I never knew this part of you,

This was a different part of us.

This was love forgery.

This was love forgery.

That's Right

I felt a certain awakening with you.
Your posture firm like a tree. You
were my roots, though wind and
storm came you remained. Carrying
one another, we grew to new heights.
My calm came from your stability, so
peaceful you showed the God in
you with that stillness. It was that
be calm and pray everything would
be okay attitude. You never lacked
for weight I could put on you, never
a branch to break, never a leaf for
a season. We were firmly rooted
together through these times of
turmoil and joy. So we would enjoy
that fruit of that long due harvest

together, that sweetness. After those long years together, we could look back, knowing it was all worth it. We could smile at each other, holding hands, with joy that we completed our purpose together.

My Eye

Society influenced the masses with propaganda

of the perfect woman, but I recognize perfect in you.

Here Together

I cuddled you, like I would never let go.

I was so vulnerable, you cried from the

openness. I said never fear, I am still

a man though I cry too. A man that won't

cry will die, for nobody ever not knowing

how he feels won't live . Let them explode,

let my love implode for you. Let's live

this entire life, moment by moment,

second by second, accepting all the

pain, struggle, and hardship with you.

I will be your lifetime counselor.

For You

I was made to drink a particular poison.

It was an awful bitterness. But you

made me drink it as I looked on

you, but you were not available. How

can I make this life worth living with

meaning if I can't place my passions

and dreams with you? Without you I

was jailed, living in obscurity, in a

mental asylum with those who

thought without reason. Can a man

live happily alone on his own private

island? Can I work these hours, days,

and years without placing that purpose

to a person? Those pearls and diamonds

are buried away deep into the depths for

me to find them for you. They bring me no

happiness but to bring you a small

expression of my love. Truly, if I can

figure out a way to harness the earth,

I would package it for you with a little

red ribbon. And if that didn't please you,

I would venture off for more planets. What I

mean is all of this is for you. Everything I

have. Everything I work for. That I stretch

for, depleting my physical and mental strength

to give. There is nothing off limits. My soul is

available to you. All I ask for is for you to

be available to me.

Keeping On

However, whenever, let's look
upon waters with each other. Until
we see every lake, every water, we
wouldn't have lived. I want to see
that stillness of water with you, to
show you how my heart is. So at
peace with you, no addition is
needed. We view the lakes, rivers,
and oceans together in silence
knowing we are bonded by love,
living as one. Can I walk these
sands holding your hand hearing
the seagulls and seeing waves
crashing against our feet? Can
my eyes meet your glance and
we feel a joy within ourselves

without a word? At this

seemingly endless ocean,

we felt a limitless commitment

that raged through the storms,

wild winds, and roaring thunders

to find that stillness again. Out of

that chaos came stability from

never jumping ship, going out

alone on a lifeboat, or giving up.

So though the ship is overrun with

water, the waves are higher than

the clouds, and the ships turns sideways,

we grew to not fear and know God has

a plan for us, and whether we live or die,

it was meant to be that we do it together.

New Season

I've been through the trenches with you.

A brutal war from both sides, knowing

you and everything that came with you.

A world of mess I had to rebuild with love.

They brainwashed you with hardships of

infidelity and mistrust. Lies and deception.

But I had to ask you, could I be your rain?

The first cycle of our trust is to wash away

the pain, let you walk through my world

washed in love that doesn't quit. Let it

soaked you, relieve you, make you

believe there is a possibility to grow

with another again. Next, your joy

will blossom again, smiles and laughs

endless as the daisies and roses in

May. And last, we will live in our harvest.

Enjoy the sacrifice of our work,

every fruit of our moments.

Be Still

In you, I found meaning. Yes, before

me men may have found that running

from here to there, from that thing to

that woman was the thing to do. But

they are behind you and I stand

beside you for that purpose. Their

hearts dashing here and there like

the wind trying to find that meaning.

Not knowing you were hidden in plain

sight, these were boys looking for new

toys to play with at best. Boy who didn't

know who they were and what they

were capable of, so they played with

meaningless things. The men knew,

to be still is for a man to truly know his

place in the world. To put his deep focus

into that, into her. We are connected to

higher sources, we are roots, not branches,

twigs, or leaves. And here we abide,

our home to grow. The streets

are by appointment and

scheduled occasion only.

All the real pleasure is to be found

here. Here on this couch we can do

whatever, however we like.

You are wanted here.

LOVE, IN THE SMALL THINGS

Selective Times

Sea and the stars, we watched it

all from a sand dune. Time didn't

exist then when I was with you.

Ate at our favorite restaurant, money

didn't mean anything although we

could have dined at the finest. Riding

on a Sunday afternoon to the park, these

moments were felt forever though we

haven't lived that long. We lived in the

ocean, though we had a comfortable home.

That dark silhouette of night with that glow

from a full moon. We forgot what the world

had going on, our souls were consumed.

Lost in you, I only remembered us.

Like That

You were my canvas, I was your painter.

I make art with massages, making miracles

out of your stresses. Oil spread across your

body down to your feet, paying special

attention to your stress points. Yes. One

of the many ways I express how much

I appreciate you. All out here, there,

providing being a real woman and you

deserve what a real woman gets. Pure

pleasure. Ecstasy without the pill. Sent

you on an emotional roller coaster just

for the thrill. Relaxation

in all ways of the term.

Owned Time

Isn't it early morning? Where you like to
be held until you fall asleep? I give you
the last of my warmth, and get up to go
to a cold job. To slave away, making the
best of it until I am free to hold you again.
As soon as you get up call me, I want to
hear your sweet voice again. That
connection lifted my spirits higher. I
came to know you again like we were
high school sweethearts, small talking,
calling each other back between long
talk sessions. Guessing and asking what
you doing. We could not be happier
enjoying these small things with each other.

A Gift

You were a breeze that carried the

warmth of the sun. That invisible

thing that made me say there's

still hope. You are an unbreakable

love that mended my brokenness.

For staying through my pain,

I give you rain, clouds full of

love that burst with

my appreciation of you.

Us, Against the World

Gone Home

They kept me at my desk with

multiples of tasks, but all I could

do is think of you. Their coils

wound around me, binding me

as I resisted the overtime. I told

them I will do what's required,

and the world will have to do

without these great inventions

because my woman is missing me.

Tomorrow will rise, but if I can't hold

my woman tonight, she will be cold.

I have what's required of my household,

but my woman needs my touch and

warmth. How can I say I am there,

and I wasn't? How can I be a soulmate

and see you as much as a distant cousin?

I will stop the world if it becomes too chaotic

with working me and say I need a moment

for a hug, for a kiss, a deep conversation,

to ask my lady how her day went, and to

know what wishes, dreams, and things

she would like to do today. I will make a

routine of this and when I die I can say

one thing. Before I served the world,

I had to serve you.

We Are Ready

We had been here yelling bring it on.

Power couple on a power trip

choosing competitors, challenging

challengers, and accepting invitations

to the most manipulative games.

Conquering conquests as one

without a question of looking back.

Let's own this and them together,

master of our destiny and minds.

Great minds think alike but our

thoughts were in harmony. Let

the world know we are here to win.

All I needed was you, all that was

necessary was us.

Took Risks

Though you were gone.

Trails of your scent flood my

senses. Visuals of your flawless

presence won't escape me.

Your whole being like nature

on a windy, sunny day. So much

peace between us, so much

fight for us to see each other more.

I was grateful and cherished every

second of our time. All the basics

were extra, all the extras were wasted.

We shared getting high from the

endless inhales from laughs, smiles,

and breath taking moments with you.

You are a mystery that cannot be solved,

but I will wonder and awe at you. You are

a puzzle that cannot be put together, but

still I will try to connect the pieces of you.

Can we run together? Feeling our hearts

beating at the speed of life at its maximum

pace. Can we face our fear together, going

into a deep forest to jump off a waterfall?

LOVE, IN THE WAR ROOM

That Existence

Changed all at once by an irreversible

force of death, divorces, and division

- keeping these reunions separate.

What an evil cause that the pause

of it brings immediate anger, pain,

and frustration. This life, this change,

wanting to live again like that time

but knowing times are a changing.

I had once knew that family of love

- surrounded by so many people --

then I don't know what happened.

Things changed. Things always

change. What is this thing called

life? Always changing but forever

remaining the same.

Means and Ends

Thought it was a myth to say

I could outgrow your love. Well,

these trees of life sprout out and

grow and we can't control them.

The battle rages against our own

desires and our lives. We bought

into this. Should we split this? All

from this new standard that I needed

to apply. These ice cream dreams are

melting away at a pace that I can no

longer keep up. At what sacrifice,

for what cause does this family

become two households? Do the

means meet the ends?

Battle Cry

A shriek from those who didn't know

their commitments. Let them scream

confusion while we roar our warrior call.

Though we failed a thousand times, I

grew a thousand times over being able

to live with you, through the mud of

conflict and water of routine. Giving

demands and taking compromises,

we could negotiate with the best of them.

Coordinating teams, we could find the

most problematic one and deal with

the worst of them. This was that stew

of life, mixing the ingredients of growth,

destruction, and commitment. Figuring

out that flavor of who or what we commit to,

destruct, and grow. Giving birth to that

death or life. We were here growing

something, but we had to destroy something

to have these things. I had to know the worst

of you to get the privilege of living with the

best of you. We both had to let parts of us

die in order to grow stronger. In these steps

of darkness, through our commitment,

we became faith warriors.

Went There

You and I had our backs against the wall. From employer to employer, from client to client. Dealing with corruption here and there. Lies told against us for our downfall. False perceptions. Kept from climbing that ladder for whatever reason. True realities in a time of uncertainty. Looking forward to your body heat at the close of day after working in the cold world. We would consul each other on these trails of evil, as we waited for the judge to render his verdict. Through trumped up charges and them offering us a plea deal on something we did not commit, we stayed true to ourselves and fought it. Risking a long sentence, I beat the case with you. The jury seeing the evidence, there was no need for fear.

Only faith, in us

Don't Worry

Darkness crept into your soul like

an adulteress. You wanted to betray

this whole life by giving up. I told

you to stay strong, the reward would

come. Though you found no reason

in the days. In the most connected

and active world, you felt paralyzed.

I was positive, that never-ending smile

would not quit at quitting time. You

had a career you built up but oftentimes

it wasn't enough to continue. Middle

fingers to it all and then plunging a

knife through your heart. Now, you

could stop searching for answers.

You would not be a part of it all anymore.

These were your fantasies.

But I kept you grounded, slicing off

just enough hope to go another day.

Told you the people, property, money

and jobs was all an illusion we could

not take with us in the end. I had the

thought that all that mattered were these

moments with you. That I will never lie to you.

That you should be bold and courageous,

never fearing. Never succumbing to the lie

that you were not enough. That others were

humans like us. Though these thoughts of

weakness plagued you, For you, I will

never give up.

Something Special

The same reality that brought me

here has taken me back. How can

men wonder about the good old times

and not take control to make them now?

Society has decided that something was

good, and men blindly went after it. Well,

I can tell you that great wealth never meant

Everything to me. But when you came through the door,

your smell hit me like the lilies of the field. I ran

up happy as a kid catching fireflies in a jelly jar.

When I got the groceries from you, I laid a kiss

on you and it reminded me of that joy of seeing

the tadpoles in that creek water for the first time.

You begin cooking and that smell made me feel

like I was back at my Grandma's house as she

cooked those huge onion filled burgers again.

Sitting at the table, I just saw so much of you,

joy on joy, as I caught feelings from your pleasing

smile, bringing that Oh My God smell to my mouth,

tasting that texture, all the while hearing your sweet

voice asking for approval. With a head nod and full

mouth smile, you knew it was real good. All there,

we made this house a home. Through the world's

eyes, it was decent. But we knew, we made

this house a home.

Closer to You

At last, another day to hold you.

Come here, lay here, let me cuddle

you, look upon you, and sex you.

Every time it's different, like riding a bike.

The wind is different, we go on new routes,

you bring me that excitement every time.

I like to play with you, wait for you to open

up your world so I can enter with mine.

And surprise you like an anniversary

But we do this every night.

Only Gain

Finding pleasure in the pain,

feeling that moment again. The

coldness of night had that

bitterness that bit like a

poisonous spider, but I provided

a certain warmth that cured you

as we cuddled. The days were

dark and full of boredom, but you

lit that excitement again, smiling like

we were new again. You provide that

lasting satisfaction I became familiar with,

I had no desire of a strange woman.

I was used to your curves, textures,

and rivers. Beauty lived here in the

darkest days with you, and now we

stand over these beautiful mountains

we overcame. Silence, as we stand looking out. Fear no more, those dark days are gone. Gentle breeze on our faces, giving relief to the end of that heat and misery. Let us breathe again in this light air. Let my light touch calm you. Let my strong hug secure you. I don't ever want to see you cry a tear for the rest of our lives unless those tears are from the love I have for you.

Your Reward

You fought for me. And that

power you have is unstoppable.

Bold. Defiant. Able to do that

which I have relentless respect

for. No matter what great accomplishments

I achieve, you were the steel support

beams to reach those heights. No

value can be placed on this, for even

on God's finest moral balance beams

your actions cannot be compared. It

covers everything, my every wrong

and my every right. My thank you

won't be enough, And I can only

be here striving everyday to provide

the best life I can give you with the

finest the world and heavens has

to offer. That would be just a small

expression of the appreciation a

Queen of your Standard Truly Deserves.

Love,
Established

Open Minded

Explosions of excitement,

I have a joy that cannot be compared

to anything. I feel like every minute

of my life was meant to lead here in

front of you. You will have everything,

sharing with you every activity that I love,

every knowledge I know, and everything

I am not. And I trust you with all of it, the

strongest parts and even the sensitive and

weak parts of me. Even in that, there is no part of

us that is not strong. We complete each other like

the forest completes the mountains, the wind

completes the air, and sleep completes the day.

We Grew

Everything had meaning with you.
That slide of my hand into your
hand created this. A warming touch,
smile, and laughter made us feel
like we stood on solid ground. We
could run on this feeling for days,
outlasting that fear of failing, we could
jump from cliff to cliff together. Even
if we had to move slower,
patience is a luxury with you.
Let me carry you until you take
those steps, can walk in danger,
or run across fire heated coals.
Our goals were a sign of this, building
a family, things to pass on, times to
remember, and stories to give. The

basis of growing through the spectacular

and uncomfortable times and situations to

make this. Eventually to pass this to a little

hand, a son or daughter to say, here, make

this life as your Mom and I did. A one not to

regret and to live with

the one you find to love.

Everybody Talking, Prove Your Word is available now.

Sign up for the no-spam newsletter for updates on new books, speaking events, and get the FREE poetry book.

Go to Clarencelockett.com and give your email address. And that's it.

Enjoy this book? You can make a big difference

Honest reviews of my books help bring them to the attention of other readers.

"If you've enjoyed this book I would be very grateful if you could spend just five minutes leaving a review (it can be as short as you like).

Go to Amazon.com Search Through Mud and Water. Find the book page. Click it. Go down half way and click the link that says-Write A Review.

Thank you very much.

ABOUT THE AUTHOR

Clarence Lockett is the author of the Through Mud and Water. He makes his online home at clarencelockett.com You can connect with Clarence on Facebook at fb.me/clarencelockettauthor

and you should send him an email if you would would like for comments, bookings, and speaking events at info@dreamcompoundprods.com